WALKS FOR ALL AGES
EXMOOR

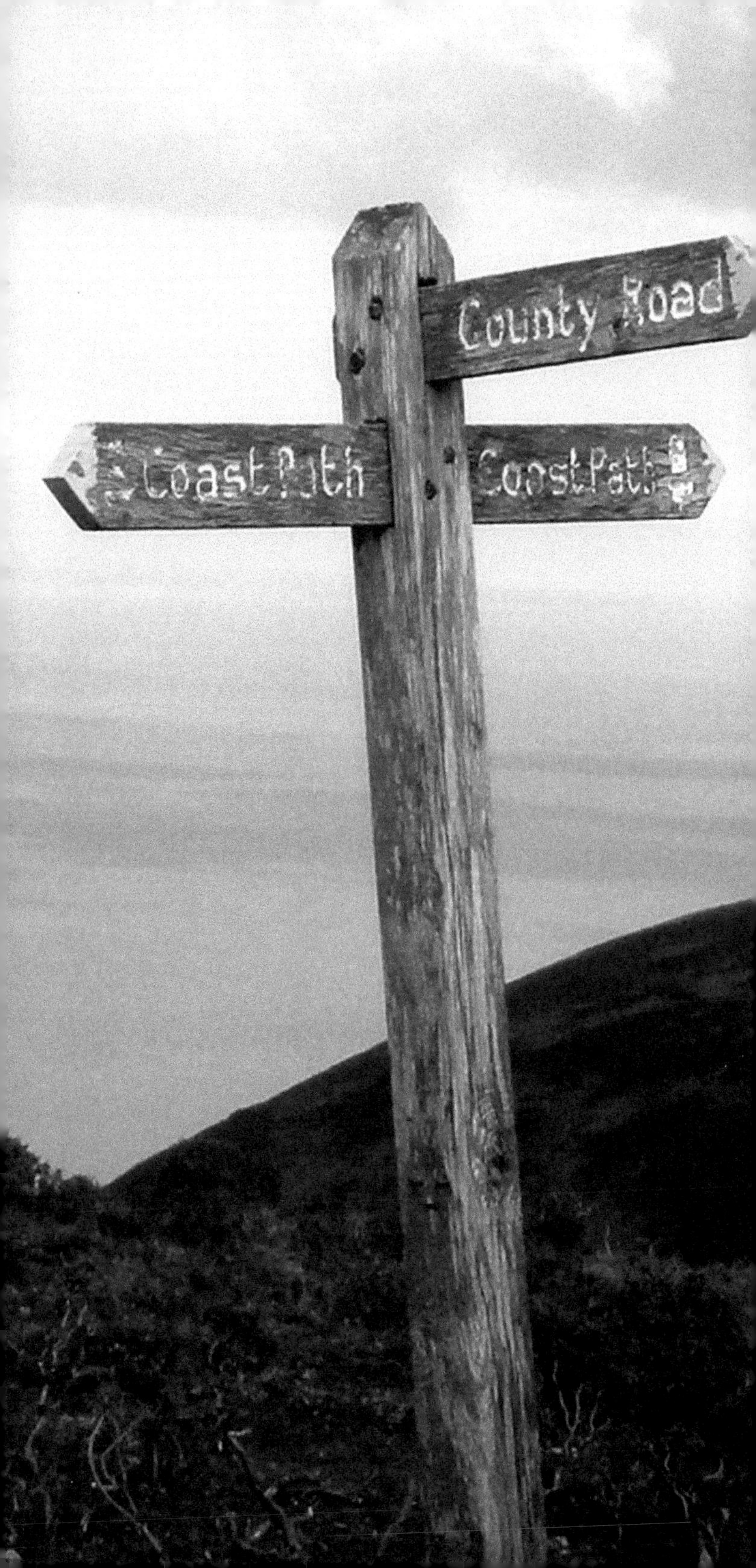
County Road
Coast Path
Coast Path

WALKS *FOR* *ALL* AGES

EXMOOR

SUE ROBINSON

BRADWELL
BOOKS

Published by Bradwell Books
9 Orgreave Close Sheffield S13 9NP
Email: books@bradwellbooks.co.uk

British Library Cataloguing in Publication Data: a catalogue record for this book is available from the British Library.

1st Edition

ISBN: 9781909914162

Print: CPI Group (UK) Ltd, Croydon, CR0 4YY

Design by: Erik Siewko Creative, Derbyshire.
eriksiewko@gmail.com

Photograph Credits: © Sue Robinson

Maps: Contain Ordnance Survey data
© Crown copyright and database right 2014

Ordnance Survey licence number 100039353

The information in this book has been produced in good faith and is intended as a general guide. Bradwell Books and its authors have made all reasonable efforts to ensure that the details are correct at the time of publication. Bradwell Books and the author cannot accept any responsibility for any changes that have taken place subsequent to the book being published. It is the responsibility of individuals undertaking any of the walks listed in this publication to exercise due care and consideration for the health and wellbeing of each other in the party. Particular care should be taken if you are inexperienced. The walks in this book are not especially strenuous but individuals taking part should ensure they are fit and able to complete the walk before setting off.

INTRODUCTION

EXMOOR NATIONAL PARK COMPRISES 267 SQUARE MILES (692 SQUARE KILOMETRES), OF WHICH TWO THIRDS LIES IN WEST SOMERSET AND ONE THIRD IN NORTH DEVON, AND IT HAS BEEN A NATIONAL PARK FOR OVER 60 YEARS.

About 7 per cent is owned and managed by the National Park Authority, with the remainder owned by the National Trust, the Crown Estate and private landowners. The National Park includes the Brendon Hills and the East Lyn Valley and is edged by the Bristol Channel.

Exmoor is one of the most attractive National Parks in England and Wales. It offers wonderful unspoilt and contrasting scenery to the visitor who likes to explore, with its beautiful coastline, moors and valleys. There are over 600 miles (1,000 km) of rights of way which honeycomb the area. These are well signposted, and whether you are a casual or a serious walker this park can be enjoyed by everyone.

Exmoor was once a Royal Forest and hunting ground, which was sold off in 1818. Several areas within the Exmoor National Park have been declared Sites of Special Scientific Interest due to their flora and fauna. We must not forget the wild Exmoor ponies and the red deer which roam the moors and valleys. The beautiful rocky headlands, ravines, waterfalls and towering cliffs gained the Exmoor coast recognition as a Heritage Coast. The huge waterfalls and caves along this dramatic coastline are enjoyed by visitors of all ages. Exmoor National Park has also been awarded 'International Dark Sky Reserve' status.

There are two main rivers which rise on Exmoor within a few miles of each other on the Chains just above Simonsbath: the Rivers Exe and Barle. They both travel across the Park and meet at Dulverton, where the river then becomes known as the River Exe and continues on to enter the sea at Exmouth. There are many attractive villages, some nestling in the valleys and others located on the coast, forming attractive small fishing harbours.

Exmoor is a wonderful place to explore the great outdoors whether you are an experienced walker or someone who prefers a short stroll. Please respect the countryside as it is a working environment and has a fantastic variety of wildlife and fauna for all to enjoy.

MOLLAND COMMON

AN UNDULATING OPEN MOORLAND WALK WITH WONDERFUL VIEWS OF DARTMOOR AND A GOOD OPPORTUNITY TO SEE WILD EXMOOR PONIES AND RED DEER.

The heather-clad Molland Common is located in North Devon within the Exmoor National Park and lies just a short distance from the unique village of Molland. The name translates as 'land of the bare hills' and the common is over 1,000 feet (350m) above sea level and clothed in heather with wonderful views across to the hills of Dartmoor. The village of Molland is located on the estate owned by the Throckmorton family. There are a number of Bronze Age burial mounds to be found on the moor and its remoteness has created a haven for herds of native red deer and Exmoor ponies.

The medieval church of St Mary stands on the hill looking over the village and has some unusual features. In the porch are the village stocks, and as you enter the church through its wonderful heavy oak door you find a number of Georgian box pews, a three-decker pulpit and elegant arches. Over 150 years ago the village grew on various trades such as victuallers, thatchers, millers, farmers, blacksmiths, carpenters, dressmakers, masons, shoemakers, shopkeepers, butchers, tailors, wheelwrights and miners. Many of these village occupations have gone, but the victualler and farmers remain. In the fields around the village Devon Red cattle can still be seen as Molland was renowned for the breeding of these cattle.

*NOTE: Parking is at Anstey Gate off the Ridge Road. Take Moor Lane out of the village of Molland across the moor to Ridgeway Cross, and turn right and park by the cattle grid at Anstey Gate.

THE BASICS

Distance: 3 miles / 5km

Gradient: Undulating

Severity: Easy

Approx time to walk: 2 hrs

Stiles: None

Maps: OS Explorer OL9 (Exmoor)

Path description: Moorland footpaths, stony tracks

Start point: From car park (GR SS 835298)

Parking: Car park at Anstey Gate, near TA22 9QT*

Dog friendly: On leads

Public toilets: None

Nearest food: Public house in the village

1. You start the walk opposite the track to Lyshwell Farm by going through a gap in the bank and following the narrow footpath in the direction of Molland as shown on the fingerpost sign. Ensure you ignore the wider track which runs parallel to the road. Continue to follow the path which bears to the left towards the centre of the common before descending to cross the top of Anstey Combe on your left.

2. You reach a junction of paths between stunted trees. Continue ahead, passing the last solitary tree on your right until almost immediately there is a fork where you continue ahead on the main track, crossing a further track before the track starts to gently descend heading towards a group

of fir trees on the opposite side of Triss Combe.

3. Do not descend into Triss Combe but bear left following any one of the small paths leading in the direction of the fir trees in the distance. Heading across the moor and passing gorse bushes you will eventually reach a sunken farm track.

4. On reaching the farm track you turn left and head up towards the boundary hedge at the top of the track and reach a gate with bridleway signs. Do not go through the gate but bear left and then right following the wall and hedge on your right side as it descends into a minor combe. Continue to follow the path as it bears to the left down towards a small stream. Cross the stream and climb up out of the combe.

5. Follow the path as it descends into a deep birch tree gorge known as Anstey Gully. The path continues ahead and you climb out of the gorge and follow the path until you pass the entrance track to Brimblecombe Cottage. Here the path becomes a wide vehicle track which you follow as it bears around to the left and you climb steadily following the track back to Anstey Gate.

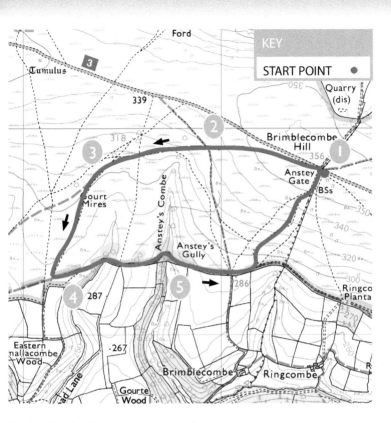

HOLDSTONE DOWN – COMBE MARTIN

A SHORT CIRCULAR WALK WHICH TAKES YOU HIGH ON THE
DOWN ACROSS OPEN WILDERNESS WITH WONDERFUL VIEWS
OF THE COASTLINE.

A beautiful walk in the autumn when the purple
heather is out. Parking is at Holdstone Down car
park which is off the A399 from Combe Martin
taking the road left towards Trentishoe.

The Exmoor coastline is a Site of Special Scientific
Interest, one of the features giving it this status
being the coastal heathland. Gorse and bracken
cloak much of the land, with interesting flora and
fauna. Reptiles like lizards and adders can sometimes be seen basking here on a hot day,
and it is a favourite place to see many interesting butterflies. Birds of prey can often be
seen flying overhead.

There were many Bronze Age settlements on the Down and evidence of hut circles,
barrows and cairns can be seen. Holdstone Down is a popular location for UFO-spotters,
who regularly gather on the summit of this 'holy mountain', and is a well-known pilgrimage
site. Near to the end of the walk you will come across a privately owned house called the
Glass Box, this is where a Dr George King had a visitation which led to his founding
the Aetherius Society. At one time the Glass Box was the society's headquarters, being
ideally situated for watching spaceships landing on Holdstone Down.

At the end of the 19th century a gentleman from Surrey bought a plot of land between Sherrycombe to the west and Trentishoe to the east, with a view to building an estate of 143 houses. Only 50 plots were sold and just two houses are still occupied.

The beautiful village of Combe Martin is nearby with its interesting main street, which is two miles long, running from the sea to the head of the valley. It also has a wonderful rocky and sandy heritage beach which all the family will enjoy.

THE BASICS

Distance: 2¼ miles /4km

Gradient: Undulating

Severity: Easy

Approx time to walk: 1½ hrs

Stiles: None

Maps: OS Explorer OL9 (Exmoor)

Path description: Coastal footpath, stony track and country lane

Start point: From car park, (GR SS 624473)

Parking: Car park at Holdstone Down (EX34 0PF)

Dog friendly: On leads

Public toilets: None

Nearest food: Refreshments in Combe Martin

1. The walk starts by taking the path on your left-hand side, by the small tree, as you enter the car park and continue to follow the path which climbs gently to the top of Holdstone Down. From the trig point there are wonderful views of the Bristol Channel and the Welsh coast. Once you have reached the summit turn left and follow the path ahead downhill and continue on this main track until you reach a junction of paths after passing between gorse bushes. At this junction turn right and continue down towards the coastal path.

2. On reaching the coastal path turn right and continue to follow the path above Red Cleave for about a mile (just over a kilometre), with views of the sea and surrounding moor, until the path forks. Here you take the right-hand path and follow the path gently uphill towards the houses to meet the road. The Glass Box is on the opposite side of the road.

3. On reaching the road turn right and walk along this quiet road back to the car park, the starting point of the walk.

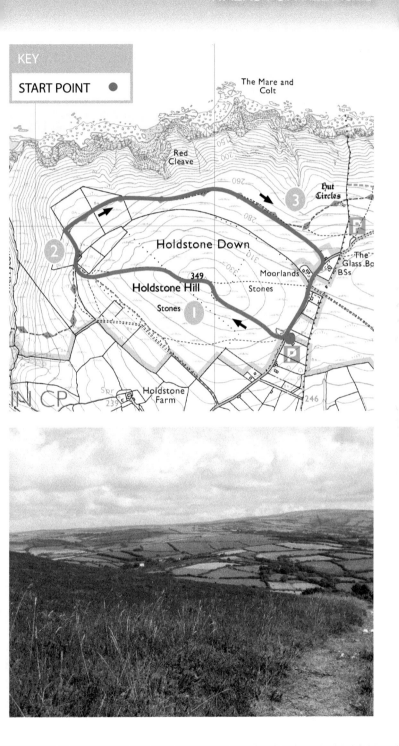

COMBE MARTIN – GREAT HANGMAN

This challenging circular walk takes you across moorland, over pastureland and along the coastal path with outstanding coastal scenery.

Combe Martin is a village located on the North Devon Coast, east of Ilfracombe, and because of the narrowness of the valley the village has principally one single long street which runs for two miles (3.2km) between the valley head and the sea. To the east of the village there are several disused silver mines with evidence of tunnels which can still be seen, as well as the remains of a wheelhouse used to lift ore from the mine.

Parts of the Crown Jewels are made from Combe Martin silver and a large part of the war expenses of Edward III and Henry V were paid for by the sale of silver mined here. The Pack o' Cards public house, built by George Ley around 1700, was funded by his gambling fortune. It was originally built to represent a pack of cards with fifty-two windows and thirteen rooms on four floors.

Great Hangman and Little Hangman is where Exmoor meets the sea. The coastal cliffs of Great Hangman (1043 ft/318m) are the highest in England and the highest point on the South West Coast Path in an Area of Outstanding Natural Beauty. From the cliffs you have wonderful views across to Wales and as far as Lundy Island.

THE BASICS

Distance: 4 miles/ 6.5km
Gradient: Undulating
Severity: Challenging walking with steep climb
Approx time to walk: 3 hrs
Stiles: One
Maps: OS Explorer OL9 (Exmoor)
Path description: Country lane, moorland footpaths, tracks, coastal path
Start point: From car park (GR SS 585463)
Parking: Car park Combe Martin (EX34 0LL)
Dog friendly: On leads
Public toilets: In village
Nearest food: Public houses in the village, village stores, cafes

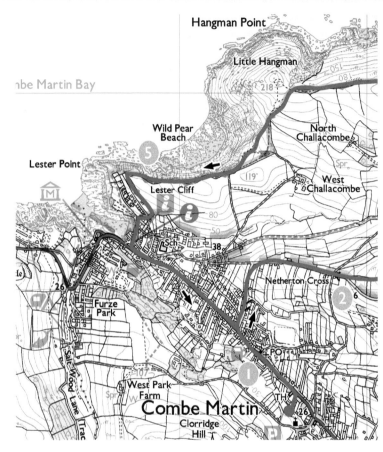

1. From the car park walk past St Peter's Church to the Main Street in the village and turn left and continue along, passing the Pack O' Cards public house on your left until you reach Shute Lane on your right. Turn right, and walk up Shute Hill, which is a long, steep climb, passing a fingerpost on your left which you ignore; continue uphill passing a further fingerpost, and shortly after passing a seat on your right, just as the road bears to the right you will find a third fingerpost on your left signed 'Girt Down'.

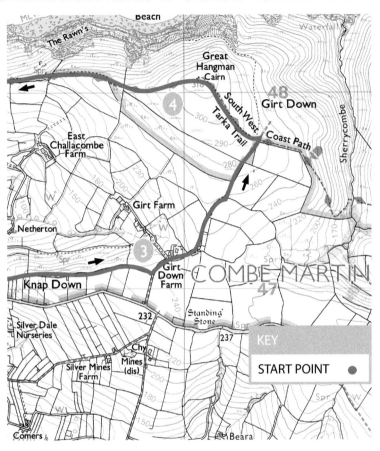

KEY

START POINT ●

2. Take this path to the left to reach a junction and a concrete road and fingerpost. Here you turn left in the direction of 'Great Hangman' and follow the track towards Girt Down Farm on your right. Do not follow the track down to the left but take the track with a hedge bank to the right and passing to the right of the farm buildings.

3. Continue past the farm, and follow the track until you reach a gate and go on to a further stile and gate with barns on your right. Go through the gate, continue

ahead across the field with a hedge and bank on your right to reach a further gate at the top right of the field. Here there is a National Trust plaque marked 'Great Hangman'. Go through the gate and onto the moorland and follow the path ahead to meet the coastal path. On reaching the coastal path turn left.

4. You then follow the coastal path all the way to the Great Hangman with wonderful coastal scenery. At the Great Hangman there is a large stone cairn, which you pass and continue to follow the path downhill towards Combe Martin. The coastal path continues, taking you towards the Little Hangman, which stands out majestically to your right. On approaching the Little Hangman the coastal path takes you around the foot of this cliff which is optional if you wish to climb it.

5. Continue to follow the coastal path which narrows and descends as you make your way towards Combe Martin. On reaching the National Trust plaque for 'Little Hangman' bear left, following the narrow footpath downhill to meet a road. Follow the road around to the right and into a car park and Combe Martin bay is on your right. Return to the Main Street and make your way back to the start of the walk.

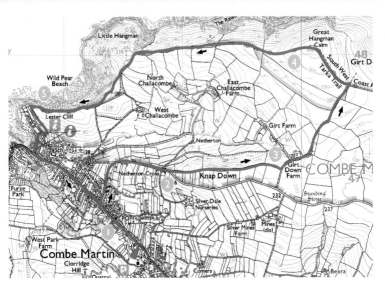

HEDDON'S MOUTH

THESE WALKS ARE BEST UNDERTAKEN ON A CLEAR DAY SO
THAT YOU CAN ENJOY THE EXTENSIVE VIEWS.

Both walks start along the accessibility route from the National Trust Heddon Valley Centre to the bay at Heddon's Mouth. The shorter walk is also suitable for mobility scooters, which can be hired at the National Trust Centre.

The longer walk takes you from the bay at Heddon's Mouth along a riverside path and high above the coast on the narrow South West Coast Path. You then follow a wide stony track which was once the old coach road between Hunters Inn and Woody Bay back to the Heddon Valley Centre. There are two steep climbs along the coast path and along the quiet road which runs down to Woody Bay. Parking is at the National Trust car park at Heddon Valley, which is off the A39 following the signs to Hunters Inn.

The scenery is the very best of Exmoor with the contrasting scenic coast, moorland and wooded river valleys. The Heddon Valley is a deep, lush wooded river valley running down to the sea. At Heddon Valley the National Trust has a visitor centre and shop.

The River Heddon rises on Parracombe Common and flows in a westerly direction towards the sea at Heddon's Mouth. The cobbled beach is only accessible along footpaths from Hunters Inn or via the South West Coast Path. Near to the beach there are remains of a lime kiln and evidence can be seen of a Roman fort which is visible on the eastern side of the bay.

Nearby is the Woody Bay railway station, which was opened in 1898 and closed in 1935. The legendary narrow-gauge steam railway of the Lynton and Barnstaple Railway is being lovingly restored by railway enthusiasts and is open to the public for short trips through the most picturesque countryside in North Devon.

THE BASICS

Distance: 2 miles/ 3km or 6 miles / 9.5km

Gradient: Some uphill climbs on longer route

Severity: Easy walking; undulating, short walk along accessibility route

Approx time to walk: 1hr or 3 hrs

Stiles: None

Maps: OS Explorer OL9 (Exmoor)

Path description: Coastal footpath, wide track and road, short walk along accessibility route

Start point: From car park (GR SS 654480)

Parking: Car park at Heddon Valley (EX31 4PY)

Dog friendly: On leads

Public toilets: At start of walk

Nearest food: Refreshments at National Trust shop and Hunters Inn

HEDDON'S MOUTH WALK

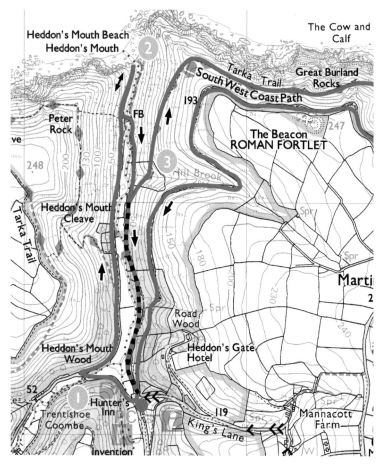

1. From the car park walk towards the Hunters Inn and follow the road to the left of the Inn. Continue crossing the bridge and reach the signed entrance to the Heddon Valley walk on your right. Follow this well-defined path with the river on your right until you arrive at the beautiful Heddon's Mouth Bay. Take time to enjoy this breathtaking scenery.

    SHORT ROUTE: To return you retrace your steps along the accessibility route; or for a more rugged shorter route back you can walk

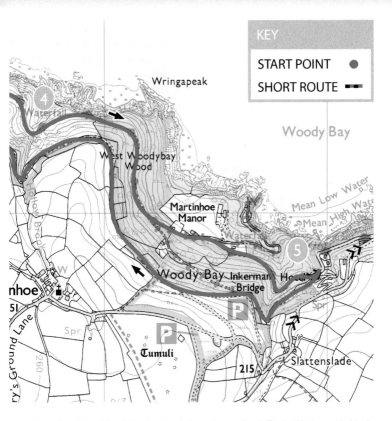

KEY

START POINT ●

SHORT ROUTE ▪▪▪

along the other side of the river bank through woodland. To do this leave Heddon's Mouth and retrace your steps until you reach a wooden bridge on your left. Cross over the bridge, turn right and continue to follow this wooded path with the river on your right side all the way back to the Hunters Inn.

2. Follow the path back to the wooden bridge and cross the bridge. Turn right and follow the path until you reach a small fingerpost marked 'Coast Path' on your left-hand side.

3. Turn left and follow the narrow and initially steep coastal path. The steep climb is really worth it as the views are magnificent all along this coastal path. Continue along the path,

which eventually takes you to a gate and into woodland before meeting a road.

4. On reaching the road turn right and walk uphill along this road. If you go left you reach Woody Bay. Continue to follow the road, passing a house on your right-hand side, until you reach a T-junction and the road bends to the right.

5. Turn right and follow the road uphill to a very sharp left-hand bend and at this point continue straight ahead through the gate to follow the bridleway along a broad track signposted 'Hunters Inn 3 miles'. Follow the clear track until after 3 miles (4.5km) you see the rear of the Hunters Inn in front of you. Just before it a track turns off to the right signposted Heddon's Mouth, but you bear left and follow the path back to Heddon Valley Centre and the car park.

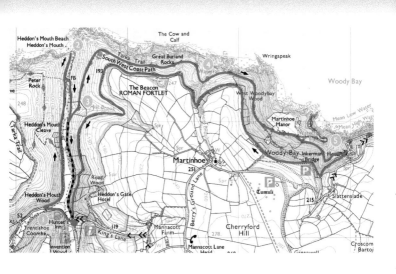

LYNMOUTH – WATERSMEET

THIS IS ONE OF THE CLASSIC WALKS OF EXMOOR FROM THE COASTAL VILLAGE OF LYNMOUTH THROUGH THE THICK WOODED VALLEY OF THE EAST LYN RIVER TO WATERSMEET AND HOAR OAK WATER AND ON TO HILLSFORD BRIDGE.

The return journey passes along the top edge of the valleys with several ups and downs before descending back to Lynmouth. The rivers, woodland and the beautiful views ensure a wonderful walk.

The quiet East Lyn River is in contrast to August 1952 when the swollen rivers caused so much destruction to Lynmouth and many homes were swept away. The walk can be shortened to four miles if required. Parking is at the Lyndale Cross car park, which is situated near the bridge over the East Lyn River.

The village of Lynmouth in Devon on the northern edge of Exmoor is surrounded by magnificent scenery. Lynmouth, lying beneath the rugged cliffs, and the town of Lynton located on the top provides a stunning location for the visitor. The Lyn rivers flow through deep wooded valleys with numerous waterfalls to meet at Lynmouth and continue across the rocky shore to the open sea.

Herring fishing was once a busy trade but no longer sustains the community, which now relies mostly on tourism and sheep farming. This beautiful scenery attracted many romantic poets such as Shelley, Coleridge and Wordsworth, who likened it to the Alps. On 15 and 16 August 1952, a storm of great intensity broke over South-West England, depositing nine inches (229mm) of rain within 24 hours on an already waterlogged Exmoor. Debris-laden floodwaters cascaded down the northern escarpment of the moor, converging upon the village of Lynmouth.

The swollen West Lyn valley and all the fallen tree debris flowed down the valley into the River Lyn through the town. Overnight, over 100 buildings were destroyed or seriously damaged along with 28 of the 31 bridges, and 38 cars were washed out to sea. In total, 34 people died, with a further 420 made homeless.

This interesting walk takes you to Watersmeet where the East Lyn and Hoar Oak rivers meet, tumbling down beside Watersmeet House, which was designed and built in 1832 as a fishing lodge and romantic retreat by the Reverend Walter Halliday, lord of the manor

at Glenthorne near Countisbury. This lodge and the surrounding woodland are owned and managed by the National Trust and it is an ideal location to stop and enjoy a cup of tea and relax. The cliff railway which joins the two towns of Lynton and Lynmouth is a must for the visitor. If you take a ride in this amazing Victorian feat of engineering you will enjoy not only wonderful scenery but a unique experience. This water-powered funicular railway was opened in 1890 and has been in continuous use since then.

THE BASICS

Distance: 4 miles / 6.5km or 6 miles / 10km
Gradient: Inclines
Severity: Easy walking with gentle inclines
Approx time to walk: 3 hrs or 2 hrs
Stiles: None
Maps: OS Explorer OL9 (Exmoor)
Path description: Riverside footpaths, countryside footpaths
Start Point: From car park (GR SS 724493)
Parking: Public car park at Lynmouth, Lyndale Cross (EX35 6EP)
Dog friendly: On leads
Public toilets: At the start of the walk, Watersmeet House Tea Rooms
Nearest food: Variety of restaurants and cafes in Lynmouth; Watersmeet House

1. Follow the path that runs beside the car park along the right bank and take the first footbridge over the river, turn right and walk along with several guest houses on your left and the river on your right to enter the wooded area of the East Lyn River and the National Trust land of Watersmeet. Follow the signs at all times for the Watersmeet Woodland walk as the path takes you from river level high above the valley and then descends to arrive at Watersmeet House. Originally a fishing lodge it is now a National Trust shop and café, where the East Lyn River and Hoar Oak Waters meet. (If you wish to shorten the walk you can return from this point on the opposite river bank by crossing the bridge and turning right onto riverside path).

2. Cross the footbridge in front of Watersmeet House and turn right, for a short distance. Just before the next footbridge turn left along a path signposted 'Hillsford Bridge' and climb steps along the valley of what is now Hoar Oak Water. At the top, bear right to keep above the stream on the right until you reach the waterfall viewpoint and then continue for half a mile (1km) to Hillsford Bridge. Turn right and walk over the bridge and keep ahead at a junction to walk along the road signposted to Blackmoor Gate, Barnstaple and Lynton.

3. You reach a hairpin bend and at this point keep straight ahead along a path signposted to Lynmouth. You are now in fact on the Two Moors Way. Go through a gate and continue climbing steadily through woodland and passing Myrtleberry South Iron Age settlement on the left, to reach open country, with wonderful views on the right across the East Lyn Valley to the moorland and then coast. All the

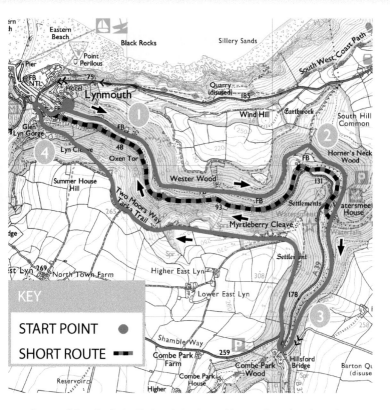

time you follow the footpath signs to Lynton and Lynmouth, and as the path curves gradually to the left along the top edge of the valley you soon see magnificent views of Lynton and Lynmouth and to the right the headland of the Foreland Point.

4. You pass through two gates in quick succession above Myrtleberry Cleave and the route now zigzags to descend steeply to cross a stream then ascends steeply, turning right at a signpost for Lynmouth. You pass the rocks of Oxen Tor and descend steeply again, going left and right through the woods of Lyn Cleave. The path then continues between high stone walls to descend back to Lynmouth and your start point.

LYNTON – VALLEY OF THE ROCKS

THIS IS A MAGNIFICENT COASTAL WALK ON A GOOD DAY WITH WONDERFUL VIEWS ACROSS THE BRISTOL CHANNEL.

The tarmac path takes you along the rugged rocky coastline to the impressive Valley of the Rocks and you return through woodland back to the town of Lynton. Lynton is located off the A39 at Barbrook. Park in Lynton at Bottom Meadow car park near the church.

The town of Lynton is situated above the village of Lynmouth, on the beautiful rugged clifftops looking out over the Bristol Channel. The two are connected by a steep road and footpath but also by the famous cliff railway built in 1890. The Valley of the Rocks lies between the northern slopes of Exmoor and the Bristol Channel. It offers outstanding views inland across rolling moorland and wooded valleys, and out to sea as far as the coastline of South Wales.

The Valley of the Rocks is all that remains of what must once have been an impressive river valley running parallel with the coastline. Gradually the sea cut into the cliffs so that the moorland rivers and streams could run straight into the sea, rather than into the larger river alongside it.

The river bed was left dry. On the north side of the valley, steep cliffs provide a home for wild Cheviot goats that help to maintain this beautiful rugged coastline. The famous 'White Lady' rock can be viewed from the road. It is formed from a hole in the rocks, which, when viewed against the sky, looks like a lady wearing a long dress.

THE BASICS

Distance: 3 miles / 5km

Gradient: Undulating

Severity: Easy

Approx time to walk: 2 hrs

Stiles: None

Maps: OS Explorer OL9 (Exmoor)

Path description: Pavements, tarmac footpath, country footpath

Start point: From car park (GR SS 720494)

Parking: Public car park at Bottom Meadow, Lynton (EX35 6AR)

Dog friendly: On leads

Public toilets: At start of walk, and along the route

Nearest food: A variety of restaurants and cafes in Lynton

1. From the car park turn left and walk up the hill and take the first turning right, North Walk Hill, situated between the church and the Valley of the Rocks Hotel. Follow the signs to the Valley of the Rocks and continue over the bridge that crosses the cliff railway and along the lane passing in front of a number of hotels. The lane becomes a tarmac path giving you views across the Bristol Channel to the South Wales coast.

2. Continue to follow this tarmac path along the coastline until it enters the basin of the valley. There are a number of seats here so that you can stop and take in the wonderful scenery. Look around you to see the interesting and spectacular rock formations, created by the weather on the mixture of hard and soft rocks. See if you can see the 'White Lady' in the rock formation of Castle Rock as you leave the tarmac to join the road.

3. You then leave this open area by bearing left and following a track along the side of the road, which is from Lynton to Lee Abbey. On your left you reach a most attractive cricket field and opposite there is a National Trust car park and toilets where you will see a small fingerpost signposted Lynton.

4. Take this path, which you follow through woodland, passing the old cemetery on your left before reaching a road. Bearing left follow this road down to meet the county road on a left-hand bend. Continue ahead (taking care) along Lydiate Lane before turning left onto Crossmead. Follow the road to T-junction and turn right to follow the road back to the centre of the town and the car park.

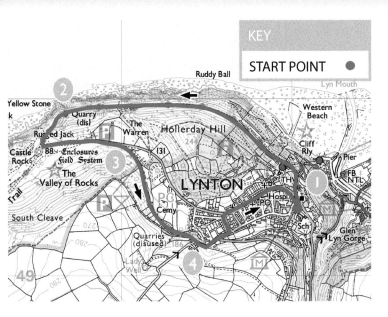

KEY

START POINT ●

PARRACOMBE – HOLWELL CASTLE

An undulating circular walk which starts in the village of Parracombe and takes you across open countryside, passing the old church of St Petrock and the motte and bailey of Holwell Castle.

Parking is in the village car park off the A39 near the top of Parracombe Lane.

The village of Parracombe is located near Lynton, in the Exmoor National Park. It is situated in the Heddon Valley and has the River Heddon running through it. The beautiful River Heddon runs along the western edge of Exmoor and enters the sea at Heddon's Mouth. Until 1935 Parracombe was served by a halt on the Lynton and Barnstaple Railway, which ran close to the centre of the village.

There are a number of Bronze Age barrows along with several other small earthworks throughout the area. The Iron Age hill forts of Beacon Castle and Voley Castle are situated nearby. Holwell Castle, which is located in the village, was a Norman motte and bailey castle built to guard the junction of the east–west and north–south trade routes, enabling movement of people and goods

furthering the growth of the village. It was built in the late 11th or early 12th century of earth with timber palisades for defence and a one- or two-storey wooden dwelling. It is thought that it was probably built by either Martin de Tours, the first lord of Parracombe, William de Falaise (who married Martin's widow) or Robert FitzMartin.

Parracombe has two churches: St Petrock's Church and Christ Church, the parish church. The old church of St Petrock stands on the moor high above the village. It was due to be demolished in the 1870s, but was saved by the writer and artist John Ruskin and others from destruction. A new church was built down in the village in 1878, and the old church, which has a completely unspoilt Georgian interior, is now used only occasionally in summer. The present building is largely the result of an early 16th-century reconstruction. The chancel and the lower part of the small square west tower, however, were built in early 13th century. The interior is plastered and whitewashed; everything is irregular and leans in different directions. There are 18th-century box pews, and a number of 16th-century benches still survive. St Petrock's is by far the most interesting of all the churches in this part of Devon; it is now maintained by the Churches Conservation Trust and is well worth a visit.

THE BASICS

Distance: 2¾ miles/ 4.5km

Gradient: Undulating

Severity: Easy

Approx time to walk: 2 hrs

Stiles: Two

Maps: OS Explorer OL9 (Exmoor)

Path description: Country paths, country road, open pastureland

Start point: From car park (GR SS 670450)

Parking: Car park near the top of Parracombe Lane (EX31 4QL)

Dog friendly: On leads

Public toilets: At start of walk

Nearest food: Public house and shop in the village

PARRACOMBE – HOLWELL CASTLE

1. You start the walk by leaving the car park onto the road and turning left. Walk down the hill to the crossroads and turn left, signposted 'Church Town and Village Hall', and continue ahead, passing the school on your right and a red telephone box before reaching St Petrock's Church (take time out to make a visit). You continue ahead towards the main road. On reaching the A39 cross over the road with care and follow the wide bridleway ahead signposted 'Parracombe Common' to where the track forks.

2. Here you continue along the path to the right signposted 'Highley' and follow this path between hedges until you reach a gate. Go through the gate and, bearing right, you descend down the field to a gate ahead and cross over the farm track and go through a further two gates. Continue to descend across the field following the hedge on your right to reach an enclosed track leading to a gate and lane. You are now in the hamlet of Highley.

3. Turn left on reaching the lane and walk over a small bridge across a stream, then turn immediately right signposted 'Footpath'. Go through a gate and continue ahead on a stony track, crossing over a small stream and climbing steadily to where the track bends sharply left with a gate on your right.

4. Go through the gate and turn immediately left to follow the path along the top ridge of the field to a small gate in the corner of the field. Go through the gate and follow the path, descending diagonally across the field to a stile in fence. Cross over the stile turning right onto farm track. Continue ahead following the farm track down to reach a cattle grid before rising to reach a concrete road where you turn left to reach the main road, the A39.

5. On reaching the A39 you cross over the road, taking care, to go through a gate opposite. Follow the path across the field, passing two stone gateposts and crossing over what remains of the old Lynton and Barnstaple Railway. You continue across the next field making for the far right-hand corner to a gate hidden in trees. Here go through the gate and continue along an often muddy path for about 30 yards before turning left through a gate at a yellow way mark.

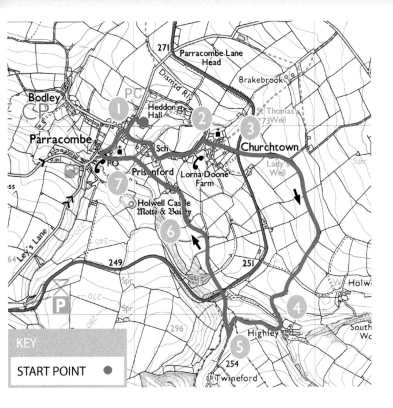

6. Bear right and follow the edge of the field over a brook a few yards ahead and then bear left, heading across to join a hedge bank on the right, until halfway down the field you see a gate with a yellow way mark. Go through this gate and the next gate and walk along the hedge-lined track, passing through another gate in front of the farmhouse. Go through the gateway with the yellow way mark and at the end of the barn turn left through the gate signposted 'Parracombe'. Continue across the field in the direction of Parracombe Church to go through a gate in far left-hand corner. Bear right over a stream and turn left to climb a stile in the hedge bank to a road.

7. Over the stile turn left and follow the road to the gates of the parish church, Christ Church, and walk through the churchyard to find an information board near to the church main door showing Holwell Castle, which can be seen across the valley ahead of you. Continue to walk around the church and rejoin the road and then follow the road uphill to reach the car park on your right, from where you started the walk.

PINKERY POND – CHAINS BARROW

THIS MOORLAND WALK OF FOUR MILES (6.5KM) IS BEST UNDERTAKEN ON A FINE DAY TO GAIN GOOD VISIBILITY AS IT IS A HIGH AND EXPOSED AREA.

The footpaths are across the moors and over pastureland. The parking area is on the roadside, off the B3358 road from Simonsbath to Challacombe near Goat Hill Bridge and the YHA Pinkery Activity Centre.

The moorland known as the Chains averages over 80 inches of rain per year and the principal rivers of the area originate from this peatland. The Barle and Exe run south to the English Channel, and Farley Water, Hoar Oak Water and West Lyn run north to the Bristol Channel. It was heavy rain on the Chains in August 1952 that caused the Lynmouth flood. The estate was purchased in 1970 by the Exmoor National Park Authority and the farm buildings were developed many years ago as an activity centre.

High up on the moors there are wonderful views as far as the sea, and Bronze Age barrows can also be seen. Pinkery Pond was created by landowner John Knight around 1830, by the damming of the headwaters of the River Barle. Knight was an industrialist from Worcestershire, who bought the mineral rights to the Forest of Exmoor from the Crown in 1818.

It is thought the reservoir formed part of an aborted engineering project in which it would have supplied a canal to power a large waterwheel planned for a site nearer Simonsbath. The wheel was to assist the operation of an inclined railway carrying iron ore from Exmoor to Porlock Weir. Neither the canal nor the railway was ever built.

THE BASICS

Distance: 4 miles / 6.5kms
Gradient: Undulating
Severity: Easy moorland walking
Approx time to walk: 2 hrs
Stiles: None
Maps: OS Explorer OL9 (Exmoor)
Path description: Moorland footpaths, pastureland
Start point: From parking place (GR SS 724403)
Parking: Roadside car park, near (TA24 7LL)
Dog friendly: On leads
Public toilets: None
Nearest food: Simonsbath, Lynton, Challacombe

1. From the parking area walk along the wide verge towards Challacombe and through the gate leading to the Pinkery Centre. Walk up the drive to the centre with the beginnings of the River Barle on your left. Just before the buildings go left in the direction of the yellow way-marked footpath. Pass through a gateway and turn right to go through a gap in the wall and head straight across the next field, where the path takes you towards the river again. Go through a small gate and then follow the path, which now runs broadly parallel with the river following the yellow marker post to its source in the face of the retaining dam of Pinkery Pond.

2. Pass through a gate and turn right to walk with the wall on your right and there is now a steady climb up to Chains Barrow (1,599 feet/487m). To visit the barrow you will reach a four-way signpost; follow the sign to the left. As you walk the triangulation point will come into view. The barrow is surrounded by barbed wire. Looking east you can see over Long Chains Common and Brendon Common while Dunkery Beacon is the hill on the skyline. If you look south you can see Five Barrows breaking the skyline and to the west you look towards north and mid Devon.

3. Retrace your path from the barrow back to the four-way signpost and go through the small gate in the wall. Walk across the field in the direction of the sign to the B3358 road following the blue marker which takes you down through a large moorland field. Ignore a gate on your right and aim for the trees at the bottom of the field. Pass through a large gate with a blue marker, turn left and follow the hedge boundary

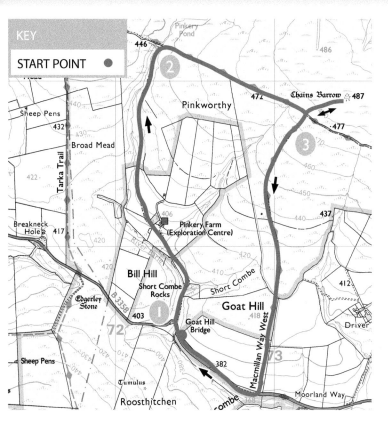

KEY

START POINT ●

on your left through gates and down fields to reach a small gate to the road. Turn right and walk along the edge of the road back to the parking area.

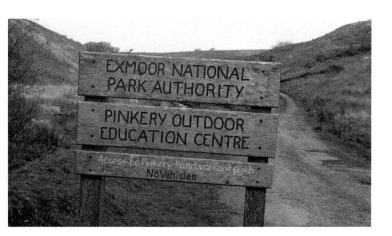

SIMONSBATH – COW CASTLE

THE FIRST PART OF THE WALK FOLLOWS THE RIVERBANK OF THE RIVER BARLE DOWNSTREAM FROM SIMONSBATH, PASSING THE RUINS OF A 19TH-CENTURY COPPER MINE AND PREHISTORIC EARTHWORK TO COW CASTLE, AN IRON AGE HILL FORT.

You return across moorland high above the valley with superb views. This walk captures Exmoor at its best. Park in the car park signposted off the B3358.

Simonsbath is situated in the heart of the old Royal Forest of Exmoor at around 1,250 feet (380m) above sea level. This was the king's hunting grounds and when the land was sold in 1818 it was brought by John Knight, a Worcestershire industrialist. He went about constructing walls, building roads and planting trees, and opening mines to find copper and iron ore, and generally transformed the area. Simonsbath is a very small village and has a hotel, public house and tea rooms. The River Barle runs through the village, crossed by a triple-arched medieval bridge. The river, which rises on the Chains, only a short distance away from Simonsbath, forms one of the most picturesque river valleys on Exmoor. Situated a hundred yards in front of Simonsbath House Hotel is a very rare surviving sawmill with 19th-century machinery. The sawmill lies close to the River Barle, from which a leat extends to drive the machinery. It was built by John Knight between 1818 and 1841 and was refurbished by Viscount Ebrington in 1898. In 1996 it was bought by Exmoor National Park Authority and was restored with Heritage Lottery Funding. It is now in the care of a volunteer group and is well worth a visit after your walk.

THE BASICS

Distance: 7½ miles / 12km

Gradient: Some uphill climbs

Severity: Moderate walk

Approx time to walk: 4 hrs

Stiles: None

Maps: OS Explorer OL9 (Exmoor)

Path description: Country footpaths, stony tracks, moorland

Start point: From car park (GR SS773394)

Parking: Public car park at Simonsbath (TA24 7SH)

Dog friendly: On leads

Public toilets: In the village

Nearest food: Public house, tea room and hotel in village

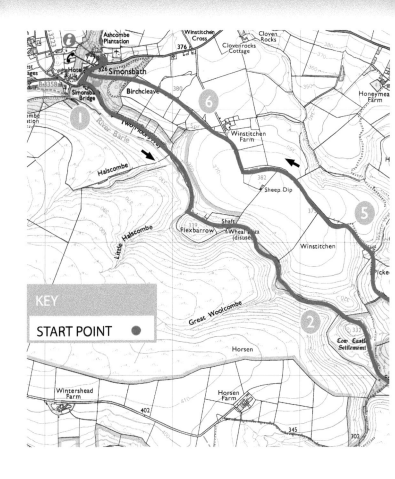

KEY

START POINT ●

1. Leave the car park and make your way towards the main road, passing between buildings. On reaching the road turn right and walk past the Forest Inn and buildings to just before the road bends to the right. On the other side of the road you will see a footpath fingerpost and a gate. Cross the road and enter Birchcleave Wood. Although it has the name of birch it is in fact a beech wood. Walk through one of the highest beech woods in England, planted at over 1,000 feet (300m) uphill to another footpath sign where the

path forks, and take the right-hand fork along a blue way-marked route signposted 'Landacre via Cow Castle', and pass through the lower slopes of Birchcleave Wood above the river.

2. Exit the wood and now walk with the river on your right for a couple of miles, passing through two gates. Where the track forks take the right-hand fork down to pass through a large gate. Continue along the footpath, passing the ruins of Wheal Eliza

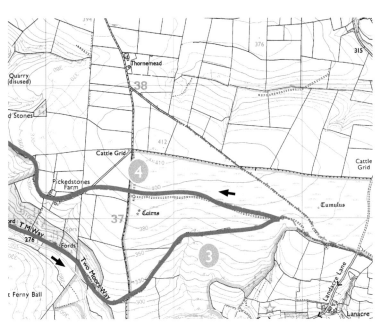

copper mine on your right, and shortly afterwards pass through a further gate. Continue along this clear track with the River Barle always on your right following blue way mark signs and passing through gates. You do have a diversion around the base of the prominent Cow Castle, an Iron Age hill fort.

3. Cross over the footbridge and follow the path ahead through the plantation to a wide track and continue along this track

through woodland to an old gate. The track then starts to climb steadily to another gate and then across bracken and heather, and away from the river. Continue to follow the track in the direction of Withypool. On your right there are fine views over the wild and uninhabited country to Landacre Bridge. Continue the steady ascent until you reach the top of the ridge, where you turn sharp left at a footpath sign to 'Simonsbath via Pickedstones'.

4. You follow the blue way-marked path along the top edge of the valley to reach a gate. Pass through the gate and continue in the same direction with a field hedge on the left to reach a further gate in the top left-hand corner. Turn left onto a tarmac road and follow it down in the direction of Pickstone Farm. Go by farm buildings and pass through a gate signposted 'Public Bridleway, Simonsbath' and follow the path to a large gate.

5. Bear right, by the hedge on your right, and follow the track through a series of gates. The track descends to cross a stream, White Water, and climbs up the other side of the valley. As you near the top of the ridge bear left between gateposts and then bear right to walk with the field edge on your right by a hedge and small plantation. Continue along in this direction to pass through a series of gates until you reach a gate that leads you to a road at Winstitchen Farm. Do not go through this gate to the road but turn left following the field edge, by a wire fence, making for the gate near to a small shed.

6. Continue straight ahead through three more gates with a hedge on the right and then bear left, with the hedge now on your left, to pass through another gate. There

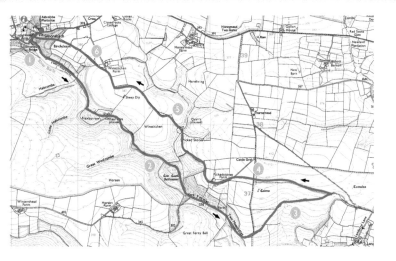

is a further gate after a few yards. Continue downhill along the edge of the field, with the hedge on your right, to the gate to re-enter Birchcleave Wood. Turn left along the path through the wood, following a 'Simonsbath' sign, bearing right and heading downhill back to Simonsbath where you can retrace your steps back to the car park.

TARR STEPS – RIVER BARLE

A VERY GENTLE WALK ON RIVERSIDE PATHS ALONG THE
WONDERFUL RIVER BARLE, CROSSING THE RIVER BY THE
ANCIENT CLAPPER BRIDGE.

Parking can be reached from the B3223 road between Withypool and Dulverton. Parking is also available for the disabled nearer the bridge. This is a suitable walk for younger children.

The Barle Valley is one of the most beautiful valleys in the Exmoor National Park. The river flows from the Chains above Simonsbath and joins the River Exe at Dulverton. Much of the area through which the meandering river flows is of special scientific interest, with ancient oak woodland and rare flora and fauna. Much of the woodland was once coppiced, primarily to provide charcoal for the local smelting industry. Both roe and red deer graze the pastures and woodland, and otters have also been seen in the river and on its banks. The age of the clapper bridge at Tarr Steps is not really known but it is thought to date to around 1000 BC. Many of the stones weigh up to one or even two tons. It has been designated by English Heritage as a Grade I listed building and a Scheduled Ancient Monument. In December 2012 half the bridge was washed away by the river which was heavily swollen by rain. The stones have now been numbered to help rebuilding should the stones be washed away again in the future.

THE BASICS

Distance: 2½ miles /4km

Gradient: Easy walking

Severity: Easy

Approx time to walk: 1½ hrs

Stiles: None

Maps: OS Explorer OL9 (Exmoor)

Path description: Riverside path

Start point: From car park (GR SS 872 324)

Parking: Car park at Tarr Steps (TA 22 9QA)

Dog friendly: On leads

Public toilets: Start of walk

Nearest food: Tarr Farm Inn

TARR STEPS – RIVER BARLE WALK

1. Leave the car park through the gate and follow the path downhill through the field beside the road. Continue along this field path until it reaches the road just above the ancient clapper bridge. Carefully cross over the steps to the road the other side.

2. Turn right and follow the footpath, which winds its way beside the river for approximately a mile (just over 1km) until you reach a footbridge on your right. Cross the bridge and turn right to follow the footpath beside the river through woodland back to the steps. Now take time to sit and enjoy this beautiful location.

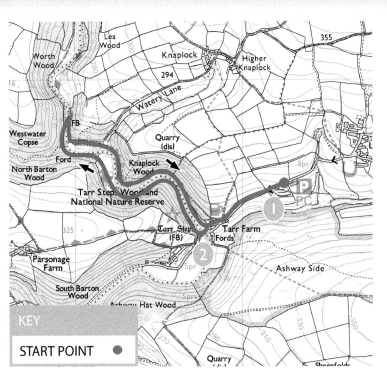

KEY

START POINT ●

EXFORD – ROOM HILL

THIS WALK TAKES YOU ALONG THE BANKS OF A MOST
ATTRACTIVE STRETCH OF THE EXE VALLEY TO THE SOUTH OF
THE VILLAGE OF EXFORD.

The first half of the route climbs over Road Hill and Room Hill, high above the valley, before descending to cross the river at Nethercote. You return along the banks of the Exe. Parking is in the public car park opposite the Crown Hotel in the centre of the village.

Exford is an attractive village in the geographical centre of Exmoor, surrounded by moorland and with the River Exe flowing through the village. The medieval church stands on the eastern edge and has a tower that is visible from many points on the walk. The church, dedicated to St Mary Magdalene (formerly known as the Church of St Salvyn), is a stone structure with a lofty tower dating from the 15th century. In the mid 19th century there were several iron and copper mines in and around the village. Exford is the home of the Devon and Somerset Staghounds, who have had their kennels located in the village since 1875. The village has a local post office and shop together with two hotels and a garage.

THE BASICS

Distance: 5 miles / 8km

Gradient: Undulating with one steep ascent and descent

Severity: Moderate but with one steep ascent and descent

Approx time to walk: 3 hrs

Stiles: Four

Maps: OS Explorer OL9 (Exmoor)

Path description: Country footpaths, stony tracks, moorland

Start point: From car park (GR SS 854383)

Parking: Public car park at Exford (TA24 7PP)

Dog friendly: On leads

Public toilets: In the village

Nearest food: Two hotels and cafes in the village

1. From the public car park pass through the kissing gate at the far end to follow a yellow way-marked route along the edge of the field, with the River Exe on your right. Go through a gate and continue along the riverside path, passing through another gate.

2. Turn right over the river, ignore the first lane on the left and turn left at the Room Hill bridleway sign. Go along the tarmac track, which soon becomes a rough track, and where the lane bends sharply to the right keep ahead through a wooden gate and along a stony track between hedge banks ascending steadily and continue, keeping by the edge of the field, with a wall and hedge on your left. Follow the field edge as it curves right. Go through a wooden gate and turn left between the hedge on your left and a wire fence on the right.

3. A gate takes you into woodland and the path climbs quite steeply along the edge of Court Copse to go through another gate. You continue across a field; take time out to look at the views to the left over Exford. Go through another gate and turn right at a bridleway sign for Road Hill, heading uphill along the edge of fields with a hedge on your right and passing through two gates. Continue to follow the path ahead through a further gate and at a fork follow the left-hand path. Go along this often muddy track, passing a fingerpost, across the top of the combe on the left. The track bears left across the open expanses of Room Hill and the stony track becomes grass. Continue initially in a straight line and then the path starts to slowly descend.

4. As you reach a hedge on your right-hand side you meet a good clear stony path that descends steeply into the valley below. At the bottom of the hill you meet the River Exe and cross the new footbridge. After crossing the bridge turn left and follow the permissive bridleway along the edge of the river and then uphill to meet a track. Turn left and walk high above the river with glorious views across the Exe to the steep bracken-covered slopes on the other side.

5. You reach Lyncombe Farm (ignoring any tracks left or right) and pass the farmhouse and go through a gate at the far end of the farm buildings and immediately go left through another gate with a yellow way mark/stile to Exford. Turn right and continue to follow the path along the right-hand edge of the field and then follow the yellow way marks across the field to rejoin the river.

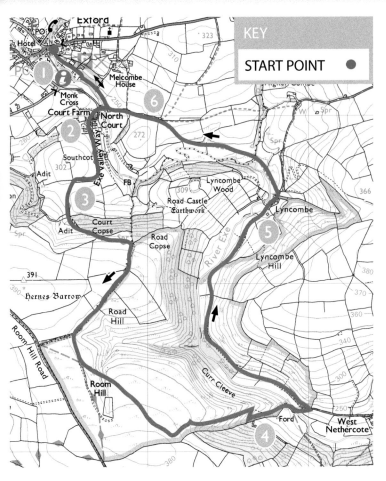

KEY

START POINT ●

6. You continue on the path by the river over two stiles and a footbridge then across the next field, keeping below the gorse through the riverside meadow. Pass through another gate and continue climbing to a further gate to a field, and follow the path as it bears right across the middle of the field to a gate and stile in the far corner. Climb the stile or go through the gate and continue down the track ahead with a hedge on your right to a gate and a footpath sign. Turn right and follow the river back to the car park in Exford.

DUNKERY BEACON

THERE IS A CHOICE OF TWO CIRCULAR WALKS WITH
WONDERFUL SCENERY TO DUNKERY BEACON, THE HIGHEST
POINT IN THE EXMOOR NATIONAL PARK.

The paths and tracks are easy walking and are suitable for younger children. Follow the B3224 from Wheddon Cross to Exford, turning right following the sign for 'Dunkery Beacon' and parking is off the moorland road between Luccombe and Wheddon Cross in the vicinity of the stone bridge at Dunkery Gate.

Dunkery Beacon in Exmoor National Park is at the top of Dunkery Hill at 1,705 feet (519m) and is the highest point in Somerset. It was given to the National Trust in 1935 by Sir Thomas Acland. Dunkery Beacon, on a clear day, offers amazing views across to the Bristol Channel and Wales, Exmoor and as far as Dartmoor. The open landscape of this part of

Exmoor is exhilarating, and inspired the poet Samuel Taylor Coleridge to produce some of his best-known works. The area is a Site of Special Scientific Interest and is part of the Dunkery and Horner Woods National Nature Reserve.

Dunkery is composed of Devonian sedimentary rock and there are several Bronze Age burial mounds near the summit. The flora and fauna can be seen at its best on this part of Exmoor, with wild ponies and red deer often being seen.

THE BASICS

Distance: 2½ miles / 4km or 3½ miles / 6km

Gradient: Undulating

Severity: Easy

Approx time to walk: 1½ hrs or 2 hrs

Stiles: None

Maps: OS Explorer OL9 (Exmoor)

Path description: Moorland tracks

Start point: Car park

Parking: Car park at Dunkery Gate, GR SS 896406 (see directions above)

Dog friendly: On leads

Public toilets: None

Nearest food: Refreshments at Wheddon Cross

DUNKERY BEACON WALK

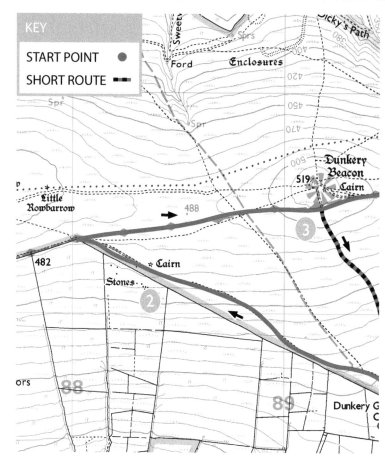

KEY

START POINT ●

SHORT ROUTE ▰▰▰

1. Leave the car park at Dunkery Gate and then take the path immediately to your left, prior to the National Trust Dunkery sign.

2. Continue to follow the rough stony track as it ascends, crossing the side of the hill,

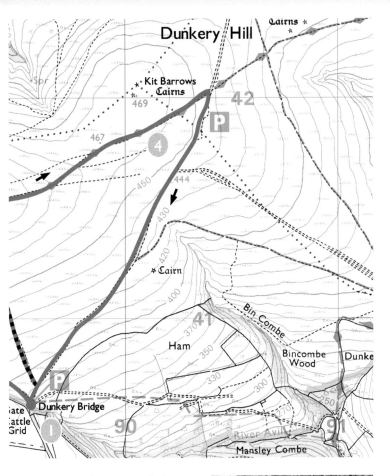

with Dunkery Beacon summit above you on the right. Follow this track, passing a wooden gate in the hedge to your left and a second metal gate before the track flattens out and you reach the brow of the hill. In the hedge to your left you will see a further gate. Here you take the path to the right to follow it diagonally towards the Beacon. Do not continue ahead on the track you were on.

3. Following the path towards the Beacon continue to ascend before reaching the

DUNKERY BEACON WALK

top and the large stone cairn. Dunkery Beacon is the highest point on Exmoor at 1,705 feet (519m). After enjoying the wonderful views from the top, and if you are following the first option and shorter route, with your back to the path you followed and the cairn ahead of you, turn right, just before the compass points marker, and follow the path that descends back down to the car park at Dunkery Gate.

4. If you wish to follow the second option and the slightly longer walk you continue ahead from the path which you have followed, passing between the cairn and the compass points of interest marker. Keeping to the right follow this path through the heather until you meet the road. On reaching the road turn right and with care follow this quiet road back to the car park at Dunkery Gate.

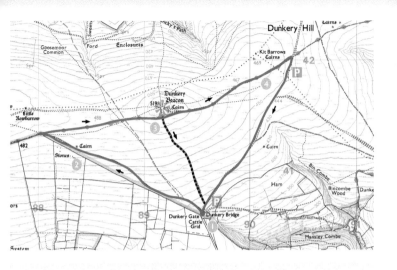

DULVERTON VALLEY

THIS WALK STARTS IN DULVERTON, WHICH SHOWS EXMOOR AT ITS BEST. THE FOOTPATHS TAKE YOU BESIDE THE RIVER BARLE, THROUGH WOODLAND AND ACROSS MOORLAND WITH WONDERFUL VIEWS.

Dulverton is located off the A396 and parking to start the walk is at the Exmoor House car park, located near the river bridge.

The small town of Dulverton in Somerset is considered as the southern gateway to Exmoor and lies between the Rivers Barle and Exe, which meet two miles (3km) outside of the town. The river then becomes known as the River Exe. The town's growth was due to the upland farming and wool trade. The headquarters of the Exmoor National Park Authority is located in Exmoor House, which was the old Dulverton Union Workhouse.

There is an attractive medieval bridge in the town which carries the road over the River Barle and on to Brushford. A number of medieval buildings still remain in the town. The beautiful church of All Saints can be seen at the east end of the town. The tower dates back to the 15th century. The surrounding area from this interesting market town is abundant in flora and fauna, and much of it is a Site of Special Scientific Interest, as is Briggins Moor situated just to the south of Dulverton.

THE BASICS

Distance: 4 miles / 6.5km

Gradient: Undulating with one steady climb

Severity: Easy walking, but with one steady climb

Approx time to walk: 2½ hrs

Stiles: None

Maps: OS Explorer OL9 (Exmoor)

Path description: Country paths, country lanes, woodland tracks

Start point: Car park (GR SS 912279)

Parking: Car park at Exmoor House (TA22 9HL)

Dog friendly: On leads

Public toilets: At start of walk

Nearest food: A variety of pubs and cafes in the town

DULVERTON VALLEY

1. From the car park walk down to the bridge and cross the bridge where you find a footpath sign directing you to Beech Tree Cross, Hawkridge. Turn right along Oldberry Lane. Follow this lane uphill until you reach a footpath sign where you continue ahead in the direction of Tarr Steps and Hawkridge. The path now takes you along the edge of Burridge Woods with the River Barle on your right.

2. Follow the attractive path as it undulates alongside and above the river for around 1½ miles (2.5km) until you reach a gate. Go through two kissing gates and onto a lane. Keeping right, follow the lane to Marsh Bridge. Cross over the bridge and, again keeping right, you then cross a packhorse bridge over a stream.

3. Cross over the road and continue ahead following the lane a very short distance uphill. You then reach a junction of lanes and continue ahead signposted 'Court Down'. Follow the track uphill, which takes you through Looseall Wood, and continue following this track for ¾ mile (1km) to meet a crossing track at the top of the hill.

4. Turn left here to go through a metal gate and then sharp right to walk up the field with a hedge on your right. You will meet a small gate and a 'Bridleway Dulverton' sign. Pass through it and take time out to visit the triangulation point on top of Court Down (1,036ft/316m). From this point you have a wonderful 360-degree panorama view showing Dunkery Beacon, Anstey Common and Winsford Hill and beyond.

5. Now retrace your steps back to the gate and walk with the hedge on your right a short distance to a gate. Go through it, then drop down the field keeping the hedge

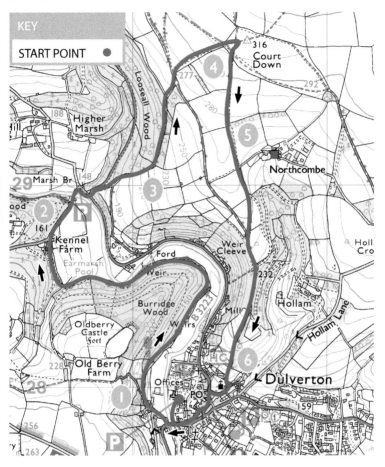

on your right. There is a gate at the bottom to enter a field with a small copse. Enter the copse, walk between the trees and cross the track to pass through a small gate leading to an enclosed track. On reaching a wider track enter the field with a fence on your left. Pass through a large gap and immediately look right to find the gate to another track. Turn left and follow the downhill path in the direction of Dulverton. The track then starts to descend between hedge banks before bearing right and descending more steeply through woodland.

6. You enter the village by the Old School House and just above the church. Turn left and then right down some steps, walking past the church to the road. Continue ahead and walk back into the village and the car park. The village is also very interesting to walk around if you have time.

WIMBLEBALL LAKE – HADDON HILL

EXMOOR LACKS ANY NATURAL LAKES AND SO THE
RESERVOIR OF WIMBLEBALL LAKE PROVIDES A PLEASANT
BACKDROP FOR THIS WALK.

From the top of Haddon Hill you descend through woodland into the lovely Haddeo Valley at Bury. You then have a woodland walk of around three miles (5km), initially by the river and later by the reservoir. Any climbing is gradual and you are off the beaten track. Parking is at Haddon Hill off the B3190 road from the village of Upton to Bampton.

The reservoir was built in 1970 and completed in 1979. It is managed by the South West Lakes Trust, and offers a popular location for walking, camping, birdwatching, angling, sailing, windsurfing, canoeing, rowing and kayaking. It is also a premier trout fishery offering angling from its banks and boats. The reservoir has been formed by the damming of the River Haddeo.

Wimbleball Lake has been nominated to be the first Dark Skies Discovery Site on Exmoor. Exmoor National Park was designated an International Dark Sky Reserve in 2011, the first place in Europe to achieve this prestigious award and only the second in the world.

As the car park is high up there are immediate fine views looking across Wimbleball Lake to the village of Brompton Regis near the lake's left bank. After initial opposition to the lake the sensitive landscaping has given it a more natural appearance.

THE WALK

1. With your back facing the road head for a gate in the top left corner of the car park. Go through the gate and keep straight, following the main track which leads through bracken, gorse and heather, climbing gently over Haddon Hill (1,165 feet/355m) with superb panoramic views of Hadborough. Continue past the triangulation point, which is a few yards to the left, for quarter of a mile (0.5km) and turn left along an indicated path through the heather. At the crossroads go slightly left and continue downhill, passing a water trough and cattle pens to reach a gate. Go through the gate and immediately turn right and head downhill. Go through the woods on what is a clear path and you will come to a gate. Turn right to reach a tree-lined track that heads downhill, emerges from the trees and continues to Haddon Farm.

2. From Haddon Farm, with the farmhouse on your left and before you reach the large farm barns ahead, bear slightly left down through a gate to follow a public bridleway sign. Follow the downhill track enclosed by hedge banks and trees. It

THE BASICS

Distance: 6½ miles / 10.5km

Gradient: Undulating with gentle inclines

Severity: Easy walking with gentle inclines

Approx time to walk: 3½ hrs

Stiles: One

Maps: OS Explorer OL9 (Exmoor)

Path description: Open country, tracks and footpaths, can be muddy in wet weather

Start point: From car park (GR SS 969285)

Parking: Public car park at Haddon Hill (TA4 2DS)

Dog friendly: On leads

Public toilets: At the start of the walk

Nearest food: None on route; cafe at Wimbleball Lake activity centre bears right and continues through a wooden gate. From here there are fine views through gaps in the trees on the right of the steep-sided, thickly wooded Haddeo Valley. Go through another wooden gate and continue down the enclosed track to pass through a gate. A few yards ahead turn right into a lane to reach the quiet hamlet of Bury, proceeding to the fine old bridge by the ford over the River Haddeo.

3. Cross the bridge, and bear right along a narrow tarmac lane which becomes a wooded track called Lady Harriet Acland's Drive. This follows the valley of the winding river and later the reservoir for four miles (6km) to Upton. This fairly level track was constructed to commemorate the devotion of Lady Harriet Acland, who nursed her husband back to health after he was wounded as a prisoner of the French in the American War of Independence. Continue along the wooded banks of the river initially to reach the hamlet of Hartford, passing the trout farm on your right.

4. You reach a bridleway sign to Upton (not the alternative route) and go through a gate of Hartford Mill. Turn left in front of a house, walking along the left-hand side of the river and then turning right over a footbridge after 50 yards. Now turn left along the other bank of the river to a gate which you go through. Keep ahead, bearing slightly right to join a concrete water authority road and continuing to a gate by a cattle grid. Go through and continue along the road, still with the river down on your left (ignoring the permissive footpath sign on your left). Continue ahead along the uphill road, climbing to the top right-hand side of the dam. Ignore a signpost on the right-hand side to Haddon Hill. On reaching the dam take the opportunity to rest and enjoy the view.

5. Immediately after the dam take a narrow path on your left and walk through the woodland alongside the lake to reach a stile and walk across to join a track, which curves left down towards the lake. Then bear right alongside it, passing through a gate into woodland.

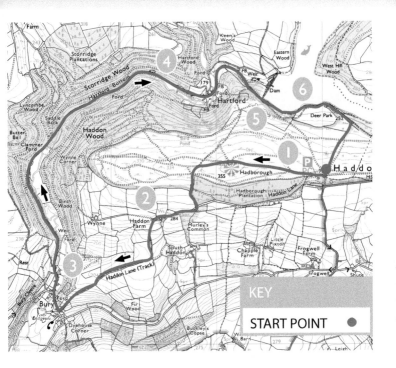

KEY

START POINT ●

6. The next short part of the walk is particularly attractive as the pleasant grassy track continues through the wood with the waters of the lake sparkling through the trees below on the left. At this point the lake becomes quite narrow. On reaching a footpath sign, marked car park, turn right and follow the footpath uphill to a crossing track where you turn right and almost immediately left to follow an unmarked and rather indistinct footpath uphill. The path levels out amongst the bracken and gorse and you continue to follow any of a number of small paths which brings you out on a road. Turn left and you will arrive at a gate and you are back at the car park.

SELWORTHY – BURY CASTLE

This walk takes you from the village of Selworthy with a steady climb up to Selworthy Beacon. The views are excellent all across this part of Exmoor.

Parking is off the A39 in the National Trust village of Selworthy next to the church.

The village of Selworthy is one of the beautiful villages on the Holnicote Estate and is owned and managed by the National Trust. Many of the whitewashed cottages have thatched roofs and the village is surrounded by ancient woodland and interesting moorland with wonderful views over Exmoor. The village was built in 1828 by Sir Thomas Acland to provide accommodation for the aged and infirm of the Holnicote Estate. Many of the buildings are listed and the tithe barn and the church and the tithe Cottage are medieval. The village church of All Saints is a Grade I listed building and the tower dates back to the 14th century. The church holds a number of interesting artefacts and is well worth a visit.

Selworthy Beacon is located north of the village of Selworthy and is one of the three peaks in Somerset. It is 1,013 feet (309m) high and from the top there are wonderful views over the Bristol Channel and across Exmoor to Dunkery Beacon and beyond. Near the top of the Beacon a number of cairns can be found which are thought to be the remains of round barrows. Bury Castle is an Iron Age fort on the hill overlooking Selworthy indicating that this area was well inhabited many years ago. Exmoor ponies and deer are often seen in the area.

THE BASICS

Distance: 3 miles/ 5km

Gradient: Undulating

Severity: Easy walking but undulating

Approx time to walk: 2 hrs

Stiles: None

Maps: OS Explorer OL9 (Exmoor)

Path description: Woodland paths and stony tracks

Start point: Car park (GR SS 919467)

Parking: Car park by Selworthy village church (TA24 8TW)

Dog friendly: On leads

Public toilets: None

Nearest food: Refreshments in the village, or in Horner or Porlock

1. Leave the car park by the entrance and follow the lane down past the church until you reach the war memorial. On reaching the war memorial turn right and walk up to a gate. Immediately through the gate bear left and follow the path down towards a stream.

2. Cross the stream by the wooden bridge and go through the gate ahead of you. Continue to follow the path ahead, ignoring the path on your right to Bury Castle. After 300 yards take the next path to your right and continue to follow this undulating path. Where the path bends sharply to the left take the path on the right signposted 'Bury Castle'.

3. Follow this winding path uphill towards a gate, keeping the stone bank on your left. Continue on this path uphill as it bears to the left and around the crest of the hill. Ahead you will be able to see the earthworks of Bury Castle on your right. Take time out to visit the Iron Age hill fort.

4. After visiting Bury Castle rejoin the main path across open countryside with woodland on your left and when you reach a gate in the wall on your left, turn right and follow the path signposted 'Selworthy Beacon' uphill. When you reach a fork in the path, take the right-hand signposted path and continue ahead to meet a junction of paths. Follow left and continue ahead towards the trees. At the edge of the plantation the path forks again and you take the right-hand path towards the Memorial Hut.

5. Leaving the Memorial Hut, head towards the road. Cross the road and follow the path which climbs up towards the Beacon, passing a path off to the left just before reaching the Beacon. After visiting the Beacon retrace your steps back to the path you passed on your left as you approached the Beacon. Follow this path, keeping left, and you will soon see fields on your right as you join the Coast Path. Continue along this path until you reach an open area with a Coast Path post on your left and a wide track coming in on your left. (If you continue ahead you will see wonderful views of the coast.)

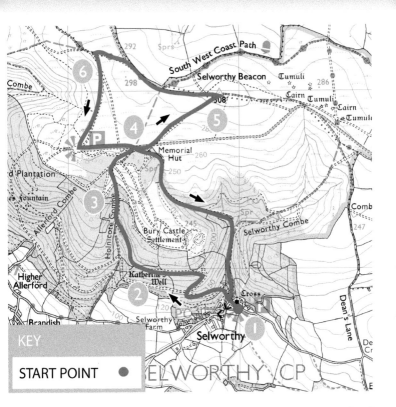

6. From this junction you take the left-hand path (in effect you double back on yourself) and then keeping right you head towards the road and a car park. Cross the road and then follow the easy access path which runs parallel to the road towards the Memorial Hut. Walk past the hut and follow the path between the trees almost to the road and then bear right to take the bridleway signposted 'Selworthy'. Continue down 'Folly Combe' until you meet a crossing track where you turn right and follow the track to a gate. Go through the gate back to the village and the car park.

HORNER WOODS – GRANNY'S RIDE

This is a circular walk from the National Trust car park in Horner Village. It is easy walking along well-defined woodland paths and tracks.

The Horner Green car park can be reached from the A39 east of Porlock.

Horner Village is one of five villages located on the Holnicote Estate which is situated in 12,000 acres of Exmoor National Park and offers stunning views of varied landscapes, beautiful moorland, a shingle beach and ancient woodland. The estate was given to the National Trust in 1944 by Sir Francis Acland. A very attractive mill can be seen in the village, which was built around 1839 to mill imported corn and is now being restored as a private home.

The interesting and beautiful Horner Woods surrounded by open heathland are a Site of Special Scientific Interest and a National Nature Reserve. Within the woods there are over three hundred species of lichens, which indicates that the wood is of ancient origin, and it is one of the most beautiful examples of ancient oak woods in the country. There are many bridleways and footpaths which crisscross through the woodland.

Horner Water, which meanders through the woodland, adds to the beauty of this area. The river is formed from the waters of Chetsford Water, the Nutscale Reservoir and Nutscale Water. Flowing in a northerly direction it meets with the River Aller before flowing into the Bristol Channel at Porlock Bay.

THE BASICS

Distance: 3 miles / 5 km

Gradient: Undulating

Severity: Easy

Approx time to walk: 2 hrs

Stiles: None

Maps: OS Explorer OL9 (Exmoor)

Path description: Woodland tracks and footpaths

Start point: National Trust car park at Horner (GR SS 898454)

Parking: National Trust Car park at Horner (TA24 8HY)

Dog friendly: On leads

Public toilets: Start of walk in car park

Nearest food: Tea room in the village

HORNER WOODS WALK

1. From the National Trust car park walk through the vehicle entrance and turn left onto the road. Continue along the road until you reach a fingerpost signposted 'Porlock'. You almost immediately cross a packhorse bridge and follow a path to the right but after 25 yards turn sharp left following in the direction of the 'Cats Scramble'. The path ascends through mature oak and ash woodland with the river below you on your left-hand side.

2. Continue to climb and follow the path as it veers to the left into more open combe with interesting views through the trees. The path continues ahead to meet a junction of tracks; continue in the same direction to reach a welcome bench. Continue climbing until you shortly reach a Y-junction in woods with a Holly Tree on your left; take the left-hand path. You then come to a fingerpost marked 'Granny's Ride' and then pass a further bench with wonderful views of Horner Valley. The path then continues to rise and bends left around the head of a wooded combe and you continue along following the fingerposts marked 'Granny's Ride'.

3. 'Granny's Ride' takes you along the edge of Yeals Combe Woods. Continue following this path through the woods, as it gradually descends downhill to meet a wide track.

4. On reaching a wide track you turn left onto the track named 'Lord Ebrington's Path' and continue downhill until you reach a further track which follows Horner Water. You turn left on the wide track with Horner Water on your right and continue along this track passing Somerset's Scouts camping ground on your right before reaching a gate. Go through the gate and continue along the track, passing over a bridge before reaching the road and Horner Green and taking you back to the car park.

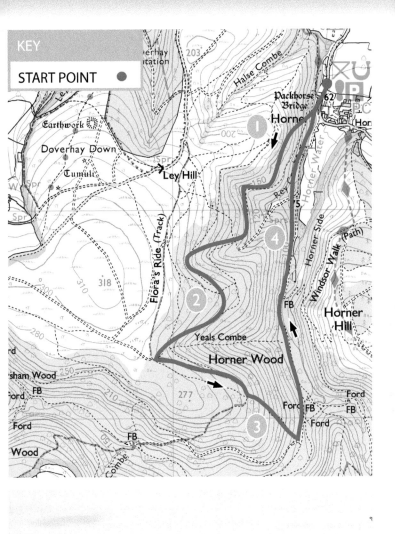

KEY

START POINT ●

WHEDDON CROSS

This walk takes you through woodland with the path following alongside the River Avill and leads you to the famous Snowdrop Valley, which is worth a visit during February and March.

You walk across open countryside with wonderful views towards Timberscombe and Dunster. Parking is at Wheddon Cross village car park off the A396.

Wheddon Cross is one of highest villages on Exmoor at 980 feet (299m) with Dunkery Beacon, at 1.705 feet (519m) the highest point on Exmoor, always in view. It is a real working community with several farms, a cattle market, pub, school, church and shop/post office/petrol station. The village is a good starting point for many walks, with the Coleridge Way passing through. Snowdrop Valley is a privately owned beautiful remote valley, close to Wheddon Cross. The Badgworthy Land Company kindly allows access to the valley while the carpets of snowdrops are in bloom throughout February/March each year. During the flowering season and if you do not wish to walk the sometimes muddy tracks the village runs a park and ride scheme to the valley.

The original Church of St John at Cutcombe dates back to the 12th century. Over the centuries many features were added including the tower in the 15th century. In recent years the church has been greatly restored and is well worth a visit.

THE BASICS

Distance: 3 miles / 5 kms with a half-mile (1km) seasonal extension

Gradient: Undulating, one steep climb

Severity: Moderate, with one steep climb

Approx time to walk: 1½ hrs or 2 hrs with extension

Stiles: None

Maps: OS Explorer OL9 (Exmoor)

Path description: Stony tracks, woodland paths, open countryside

Start point: Car park at Wheddon Cross (GR SS 923387)

Parking: Car park at Wheddon Cross (TA24 7DU)

Dog friendly: On leads

Public toilets: In Wheddon Cross at start

Nearest food: Wheddon Cross: tearooms and public house

WHEDDON CROSS WALK

1. Leave the car park with the bus shelter on your right and turn left to pass the local public house and cross straight over the crossroads, taking care, and continue ahead to reach the war memorial. Bear to your right and continue towards Cutcombe, and on reaching the school bear to your left.

2. Follow the road and after a short distance the road bears round to the right; here you take the bridleway on your left signposted to Dunkery Beacon. Continue along the track to meet a gate which takes you into a field; follow the path ahead with the hedge on your right to a gate by a lane.

3. Cross straight over to a lane to Raleigh Manor and continue to follow this lane down to reach a gate and a signpost to Draper's Way. Take this bridleway and follow the path down into the valley with a stream on your right. Continue to follow the path, passing through two gates and ignoring any path coming in from the left and right, until just before reaching a road you meet a junction of paths. Take the path to your right and follow the path which takes you downhill with a narrow lane below you on your left.

4. You then reach the road with Snowdrop Valley across the road. During the flowering season (February and March) you are able to take the permissive path, obeying local signs to view the carpet of snowdrops in this picturesque valley. If not taking the half-mile (1km) extended loop you bear right and continue to follow the path uphill, ignoring paths to the left and right until you near the top of the hill, where you go right along a sunken path which leads to the main road.

5. Cross over the main road with care and take the forest track opposite signposted 'Ashwell Lane'. Follow the forest track uphill passing the entrance to Luckwells Wood on your right and Quarry Woods to your left until you reach a gate. Go through the gate and bear left following the boundary, passing the first field gate on your left, to the top of the field to reach another gate and a track. Join the track and then turn right onto the road. Continue along the road, passing Cutcombe church, ignoring the bridleway on your right to reach a fork in the road.

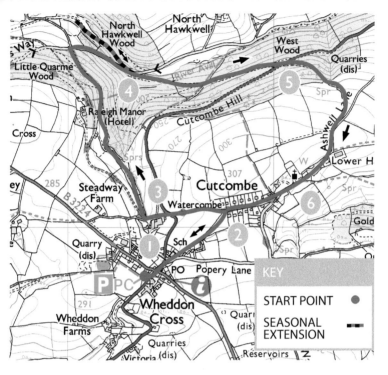

6. Take the left-hand fork and continue to the next road junction where you turn right. Follow ahead along the road to reach the school ahead, where you bear left to the main road. Continue ahead to the crossroads and the car park from where you started the walk.

DUNSTER – TALLEST TREE WALK

BOTH THESE WALKS ARE ON THE CROWN ESTATE IN EXMOOR NATIONAL PARK. THE LONGER WALK TAKES YOU FROM THE INTERESTING DUNSTER VILLAGE AT GALLOX BRIDGE, THROUGH WOODLAND AND ALONG FOREST TRAILS TO THE ARBORETUM WHERE THE TALLEST TREE IN ENGLAND CAN BE FOUND.

It returns by way of an Iron Age hill fort with magnificent views. Parking is in Dunster at Gallox Bridge car park which is off the A396 by the Foresters Arms. Alternatively at Nutcombe car park there is disabled parking and the 'Tallest Tree Trail' is suitable for wheelchairs and children's buggies.

Dunster village is on the edge of Exmoor National Park and is a medieval village with a number of listed buildings. Dunster grew in wealth through the wool trade and the weaving of cloth. Dunster Castle, located on the wooded hillside overlooking the Avill Valley and the Bristol Channel, became the country home of the Luttrell family, who have lived there for 600 years, and is now owned by the National Trust. The Dunster estate of over 9,000 acres is managed by The Crown Estate, who acquired it in the 1950s. The estate has eighteen tenant farms and over 2,000 acres of commercial woodland. A network of trails provides interesting walking, some with spectacular views across Exmoor and beyond together with diverse flora and fauna. These two walks give you the opportunity to see the tallest tree in England, a Douglas fir that has grown to 197 feet (60m). It was planted by Luttrell family in 1876 together with a number of other exotic and giant trees.

THE BASICS

Distance: 4¼ miles/ 7km or 2½ miles / 4km
Gradient: Undulating
Severity: Easy walking, with gentle ascents and descents
Approx time to walk: 2 hrs or 1 hr
Stiles: Two stiles on longer walk
Maps: OS Explorer OL9 (Exmoor)
Path description: Forest tracks, quiet roads and paths
Start point: Car park at Gallox Bridge (GR SS 989432)
Parking: Car park at Gallox Bridge (TA24 6SR)
Dog friendly: On leads
Public toilets: In Dunster
Nearest food: A variety of cafes and public houses in Dunster

1. From the car park turn left and walk between cottages towards Gallox Bridge. (Gallox Bridge dates from the 15th century and once carried packhorses which brought fleeces to Dunster market.) Cross the bridge and continue ahead to the junction of tracks and information board. On reaching the information board bear right, taking the track signposted 'Bats Castle', and follow  the track up the slope and continue ahead climbing gently to where the track forks. Bear right and continue ahead on this track, ignoring a further track off to the right. At a sharp bend you will reach a track to the right; take this track and after a short distance you will reach the Vinegar Hill viewpoint to your right with views over the Avill Valley. Take time out to visit the viewpoint and sit and enjoy the wonderful views.

2. Retrace your steps back to the track and continue ahead, passing a carved wooden bear, until you meet a junction of tracks. Turn right and follow the track as it winds downhill and meets Broadwood Road. On reaching the road turn left, then continue along the road until you reach a turning on the left. This is the start of the 'Tall Tree Trail' which you will follow through the magnificent trees.

   Shorter walk: Follow the trail up and back to rejoin Broadwood Road and you retrace your steps back to Gallox Bridge.

3. On reaching a group of seats and a wood carving rejoin Broadwood Road by turning left onto the road at a direction post and continue along the road until you reach a track to the left by a 'Wessex Water' sample tap. Turn left onto this track and follow it uphill into the woods until you reach a junction of tracks. Turn left and follow the track downhill to meet a track at the bottom. Turn right and continue ahead along the track

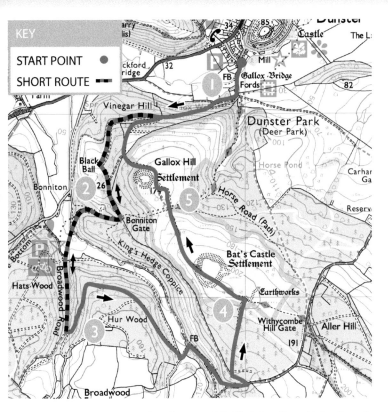

until you reach a gateway and a stile on your left. Climb the stile and follow the path across the field to another stile, which you climb, and then cross a wooden bridge.

4. Turn right and continue to follow the forest track steadily uphill, ignoring any paths off to the right and the first track to the left. As the track bends sharply left, you shortly reach a junction on your left. Turn onto this path and continue to follow ahead until the track shortly takes you through a gap in a wall and continues uphill through the forest to a tall gate. Go through the gate and onto open heathland and a footpath signposted 'Bats Castle' to the left. Follow this footpath uphill to the hill fort, where there are spectacular views of Exmoor, the Quantocks and the South Wales coast, and then continue to follow the path downhill to a fingerpost.

5. Here you continue downhill, following the track ahead signposted 'Bats Castle Circuit' to a tall gate in the woods. Go through the gate and bear right at a fingerpost and follow the track downhill through the forest to a Y-junction. Bear right here and continue to follow the track towards Dunster, passing the information board and cottages to return to Gallox Bridge.

MINEHEAD – JIM'S PATH

A SHORT WALK ALONG WOODLAND PATHS AND OPEN COUNTRYSIDE WITH SOME GENTLE UPHILL CLIMBS AND WONDERFUL VIEWS OF THE TOWN OF MINEHEAD, THE HILLS AND THE COAST BEYOND.

There are a number of seats on the route which enable you to relax and enjoy the views. Parking is off North Hill Road out of Minehead, with parking available near to the first cattle grid.

The coastal town of Minehead lies on the northern edge of Exmoor National Park. There was a small port at Minehead in the 14th century, which grew over the years to become a major trading centre in medieval times. As trade transferred to larger ports in the 20th century, pleasure steamers then brought tourists into the port and Minehead developed into a very popular holiday destination. Today the town is the home of a Butlin's Holiday Park which increases Minehead's seasonal tourist population by several thousand. The railway was opened in 1874 and closed in 1971 but has since reopened as the West Somerset Railway with steam trains running from Minehead to Bishop Lydeard.

Minehead is the starting point of the South West Coast Path National Trail, the nation's longest long-distance countryside walking trail, which winds its way around the coastline of Devon and Cornwall and all the way to Poole in Dorset. The start is marked by a huge sculpture of a pair of hands holding a map. North Hill is where Exmoor National Park begins and it dominates the town of Minehead with its green slopes which can be seen for miles around.

THE BASICS

Distance: 2¼ miles / 4km

Gradient: Undulating

Severity: Easy walking, gentle ascents and descents

Approx time to walk: 1½ hrs

Stiles: None

Maps: OS Explorer OL9 (Exmoor)

Path description: Stony tracks, woodland paths, open countryside

Start point: Car park at North Hill (GR SS 959469)

Parking: Car park at North Hill (TA24 5LB)

Dog friendly: On leads

Public toilets: None

Nearest food: Refreshments available in Minehead

1. You start the walk by taking the wide track that leads off to the left and continue along this track for a short distance until you meet a junction of paths. Here you bear right and follow the track to where the tracks fork and take the right-hand fork, following the stony track which you climb up with wonderful views of the town of Minehead to your left.

2. Continue along the stony track to reach a crossing of tracks near a small 'Wessex Water' reservoir and a seat. Turn left and follow the level track with the reservoir fence on your left and continue along this path ('Jim's Path') as it narrows and bends to the right. You continue to gently climb the upper slopes of Woodcombe before you reach a wide bridleway at a junction of paths.

3. Turn left along the bridleway downhill and after a short distance follow the path as it bends around to the left. Continue along this stony path as it takes you down through the woods and cross a small stream which

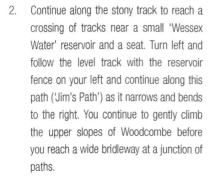

flows across the path ahead of you. Continue down the track with a stream on your left until you reach a fingerpost on your left. Turn left in the direction of 'Minehead' and follow 'Peggy's Path' as it winds gently uphill around the ridge. The path then levels out with good views to the west. Continue along the path until you reach a five-way crossing of paths where you continue straight ahead to the crest of the hill in the direction of 'Hill Road'.

4. At the crest of the hill you turn left and continue uphill along this winding path onto the valley side and walk past the seat that commemorates Peggy Pearson and continue ahead on the path, climbing gently and following the path as it bends to the right to a junction of paths. At the junction turn right and rejoin your outward path, and after a short distance at the next junction bear left and follow the path along the edge of the fields on your right to reach the road and the start of the walk.

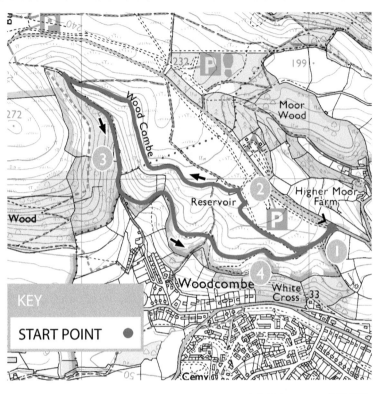

KEY

START POINT ●

PORLOCK WEIR – CULBONE

This circular walk follows the coast path, which is slightly inland here and has wonderful views across the channel, and you return over moorland and through woodland. Parking is in Porlock Weir off the B3225.

Porlock Weir lies west of Porlock and is an old fishing harbour with a small community which has grown around the harbour. The harbour has existed for over a thousand years and still has a number of fishing boats and yachts. In the 18th and 19th centuries coal from South Wales was the main import. The picturesque harbour which nestles beneath the hills of Exmoor has many thatched cottages that are very old, some of which date back to the 17th century and are Grade I listed. The historic Ship Inn is located on the harbour with wonderful views across the channel to Wales.

Culbone Church of St Beuno in the village is said to be the smallest parish church in England and is another Grade I listed building, with the churchyard cross being Grade II listed. The church seats only 30 people and dates back to the 13th century. It was used as a location for a television version of Lorna Doone.

THE WALK

1. Leave the car park and head for the coast path, which can be found signposted between the Ship Inn and Anchor Hotel. Continue to follow the path across fields until you reach a lane. Here you continue along the coast path to your right until you reach the toll gate and then follow the path to the right of the toll house and make your way on the coast path, which winds its way up through the woods to Culbone Church. On reaching Culbone Church take time out to visit this quaint little building.

THE BASICS

Distance: 5 miles / 8km

Gradient: Undulating

Severity: Undulating but good tracks with one steep climb

Approx time to walk: 2 hrs

Stiles: None

Maps: OS Explorer OL9 (Exmoor)

Path description: Coastal path, open countryside

Start point: Car park at Porlock Weir (GR SS 863480)

Parking: Car park at Porlock Weir (TA24 8PD)

Dog friendly: On leads

Public toilets: Start of walk

Nearest food: Refreshments at Porlock Weir

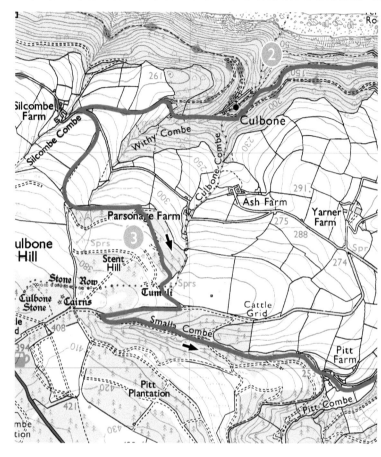

2. On leaving the church trace your steps back to rejoin the coast path and follow the path uphill through the woods which surround Culbone Church, and at the first Y-junction take the left fork, the alternative coast path signposted 'Silcombe B&B' continuing ahead to meet a lane just before Silcombe Farm. Turn left onto the lane and follow the lane for a short distance before turning right onto a stony concrete track with a fingerpost directing you to Culbone Inn. Follow this steep track up the hill towards the fir tree plantations and continue ahead to meet a road.

3. On reaching the road turn left, and continue on the road to the first signposted path on your right. Take this footpath/bridleway, which gradually goes down into the combe to a stream and a small ford. Cross the ford and take the path with the stream on your left and walk down to reach the buildings of Pitt Farm.

4. Follow the path down the farm drive with the stream over on your right before meeting

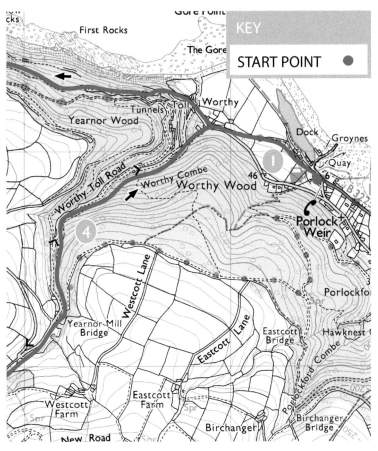

KEY

START POINT ●

a Y-junction of roads. Take the right fork and shortly take the footpath to your right over a bridge which goes left uphill into the woods, with the stream on your left, and continue to follow the path as it bends sharply to the left and you will find a left-hand path to walk down Worthy Combe, with the stream now on your right. Follow this path, which takes you downhill through the woods to reach a road. On reaching the road turn right and then almost immediately left to follow the Coastal Path back to Porlock Weir, which is retracing your outward journey.

ABOUT THE AUTHOR

Exmoor is my most favourite part of England for walking. It offers you such beautiful countryside, with its moors and valleys and exciting coastline. Over many years whilst running a walking holiday company with my husband Graham, we have taken many hundreds of people walking on Exmoor to show them how diverse, beautiful and challenging Exmoor can be.

The walks I have selected for this book will give you and your family a taste of all that Exmoor has to offer and I hope that it will encourage you to return over and over again as there is so much to see and do on Exmoor.

Every time I walk on Exmoor with the family we are amazed at the wonderful ever changing scenery, together with the opportunity to see Red Deer and the famous Exmoor ponies. I hope that you will enjoy walking on Exmoor too!

Sue Robinson
www.bathwestwalks.com